The Reign of Jesus Christ. a Sermon, Delivered at Concord

by Nathaniel West Williams

Address:
HardPress
8345 NW 66TH ST #2561
MIAMI FL 33166-2626
USA
Email: info@hardpress.net

Williams - Reign of Jesus Christ - 1827

REV. MR. WILLIAMS'

ELECTION SERMON

1827.

THE REIGN OF JESUS CHRIST.

A

Sermon,

DELIVERED AT CONCORD,

BEFORE

His Excellency the Governor,

THE HONORABLE COUNCIL,

AND

BOTH BRANCHES OF THE LEGISLATURE

OF THE

STATE OF NEW-HAMPSHIRE,

JUNE 7, 1827.

BY REV. NATHANIEL W. WILLIAMS, A. M.
Of the Baptist Church in Concord, N. H.

CONCORD:
PRINTED BY JACOB B. MOORE.
For the State.
1827.

State of New-Hampshire.

In Senate, June 7th, 1827.

Resolved, That a Committee be appointed to wait on the Rev. Mr. Williams, and present to him the thanks of the Legislature, for his able and ingenious discourse delivered this day, before his Excellency the Governor, the Honorable Council, and both branches of the Legislature, and request of him a copy for the press.

S. DINSMOOR, Jr. Clerk.

A true Copy—Attest

B. B. FRENCH, Assistant Clerk.

In the House of Representatives, same day.

Read and concurred—

SAM'L. D. BELL, Clerk.

Sermon.

Thy kingdom come.—MATT. vi. 10.

When we recede to the period just preceding the Reformation, we are surrounded with darkness and gloom. Science scarcely gave a sufficient light to indicate its existence, and the Bible, that book of books, was only to be found in the hands of a superstitious and oppressive priesthood. Every fraud which ingenuity could devise, and every fetter which power could forge, were employed to delude the people and hold the mind of man in the most abject slavery. Oppressed and deceived, and made to believe that salvation was at the disposal of the pope and his legions, the multitude was satisfied with the domination that gave direction to their sentiments and practice. But there were a few, a secluded and unknown few, whom God had taught by his spirit and who preferred the caverns of the earth, with freedom of conscience, to all the grandeur of palaces, enslaved to the superstition and borne down under the oppression of cardinals and monks.—That secluded few sent up their united cries to the throne of Jehovah from dens and caves until a prayer hearing God came down to deliver and to bless them. Wickliffe, emboldened for the truth in Britain, was succeeded by Luther and Melancthon in Germany, Zuinglius in Switzerland, Calvin in Geneva, and several others who were distinguished in their day, each putting forth his might for the cause of Truth, and the Salvation of the world. God heard their cries, and nerved their arms in the holy contest. The spell was broken, impervious darkness yielded to the spreading light of the sun of truth. A severe conflict ensued.—The enemy was powerful, but the cause was the cause of God and must prevail. With an extensive survey, behold the march of truth through the lapse of three hundred years. How astonishing the rapidity! What wonderful success has God given to the preaching of the Cross and the free circulation of the scriptures without note or comment! And who is there present, but can see a change and improvement which has been constantly advancing for the last thirty years, still more astonishing and delightful to the mind of every philanthropist? How intimately political revolutions are connected with those of the church, it is easy to see in the history referred to. The mind, released from the bondage of superstition, pursues its own enquiries. Every new discovery is sure to lead to another, and so by an indefinite progression, necessarily leads to improvement in every relation of life. If improvements in the church tend to prepare mankind for advancement in their civil and political condition, so does advancement in the civil and political condition of men, prepare them for improvements in their moral and religious situation.

Men to pursue their own best course, must possess that stimulus to action which a state of freedom alone can give, and every revolution which facilitates the march of liberty, we hail as tending to place mankind in that state in which they will feel it to be their privilege to put forth the might of their moral and intellectual strength to promote the happiness of the world.

But man is too wicked, too much given to licentiousness to make the best improvement of his advantages, without a greater moral influence than he naturally possesses. Hence while nations are improving in their civil and political conditions, they must be enlisted as subjects of the Prince of peace. Governments may be established, and laws may be enacted and executed, but, if fear be the only passion which is affected, the benefit arising from civil and political institutions will be small. It is a moral influence, which possesses the only efficient power, and this influence can be produced and successfully exerted only by the authority of the divine Lawgiver and Ruler. Aware of the necessity of such a power to form the christian character and renovate the world, Jesus taught his disciples the prayer contained in the text, *Thy Kingdom come.*

To the continued use of this petition, some have objected, believing that it was designed to be limited to the first introduction of the gospel dispensation. But I am inclined to believe that it is as appropriate *now* as it was *then*, and that it will be appropriate as long as the church of Christ shall need an increase of her number and moral power. The fitness of this prayer will appear still more evident, if we understand the text as translated by the learned Mr. Campbell, who renders it "Thy *reign* come," indicating, not so much the subjects composing the kingdom, as the authority and influence of the king himself in giving effect to his laws as the basis of his government. Hence the text may be paraphrased, Let thy government be established, thy power be exerted, and thy influence be every where spread. This, the whole Israel of God pray for, as the consummation of their hopes and faith. And what may we expect, rather, what may we not expect, while this prayer is ascending from ten thousand hearts in unison before the throne of Jehovah, but a speedy fulfilment of predictions of glory and perfection of peace and joy to the world.

On this anniversary, which is dear to the citizens of this State, I propose to call your attention to the reign of Jesus Christ and to explain the nature of his kingdom, as contrasted with the kingdoms of this world. The nature of this kingdom, we may learn by considering,

I. *Its origin.*

This we are taught by the Son of God, whose language is, " My kingdom is not of this world." It did not originate in this world, and is not modelled and controlled by the genius and habits of this world. Hence, the reign of Jesus is essentially different from the reign of any other Monarch. It is true that earthly governments are reared to afford to mankind a shelter from the many evils to which a people without rulers would be necessarily exposed and subjected. But history teaches us, that that which ought to afford a covert from the blast of oppression, has in many instances been converted into an engine of cruelty, by which the people have been filched of their earnings and robbed of their freedom. But however the design of government has been perverted and detroyed, it is certain that its intention as instituted by Jehovah, is the preservation of the natural rights of men, whereby they may improve and enjoy life in " all godliness and honesty." Had the first king of the Hebrews sought the promotion of these objects among his subjects, the purposes of government would have been answered in the reign of Saul; but when grandeur, induced by a love of power, bore an unrestrained sway in his mind, he could burthen the people with exactions, and even sacrifice the life of David, to his pride and thirst for dominion. How often have the reigns of earthly princes originated in conquest, in fraud and in the triumph of the powerful over the feeble! Within a single century, how many kingdoms have been created which received their existence and were shaped by the hand of despotism and pride, and how little justice or virtue has attended their rise and progress! While the constitutions of most governments are laid in ambition and tyranny, the foundation of Emanuel's reign is laid in righteousness and benevolence. "All power," was committed to his hands, because he could be safely trusted with it, and "all things are put beneath him, because he will make them subservient to the reign of righteousness and true holiness." In Jesus, all the qualities requisite to an empire of benevolence are concentrated, as, perfect purity, consummate wisdom, and almighty power. Hence his reign must be a government of the greatest security and happiness to all who live under it. It is true that his empire is gained by victory, but it is the victory of love. He is the redeemer of sinners, and in the exercise of his mediatorial authority, he is ever giving proof that he is unchangeable in his love to all who obey him, and that he is worthy to reign. In consequence of what he did in obedience to the law and what he suffered in his death upon the cross, "God hath highly exalted him and given him a name which is above every name, that at the name of Jesus, every knee should bow, of things in heaven and things in earth and things under the earth, and that every tongue should confess that Jesus Christ is Lord to the glory of God the Father." This is the occasion of the "heavenly host crying with loud voice, Worthy is the Lamb that was slain to receive power, and riches, and wisdom, and strength, and honor, and glory, and blessing."

As the reign of Jesus originated in goodness, so the laws of his realm are correspondent in benevolence.

Earthly governments which Jehovah instituted, and adapted to the highest earthly advantages and happiness, are often rendered abodes of wretchedness and disgrace by unjust and oppressive laws. But throughout the whole administration of Jesus Christ, his procedure is directed by laws of rectitude, wisdom, and goodness.—Nothing is prohibited but what would be productive of evil, nor any thing required but what a regard to the welfare of every subject demands.—"The law of the Lord is perfect, converting the soul, the testimony of the Lord is sure making wise the simple, the statutes of the Lord are right rejoicing the heart, the commandment of the Lord is pure enlightening the eyes." How different from this are earthly governments! Their legislatures, not unfrequently contain corrupt aspiring men, and sometimes are wholly under the controul of an influence which disregards the prosperity and happiness of the public; the statutes which they frame look more to the aggrandizement of a few, than to the good of the many.—In kingdoms, the people have groaned under oppressive laws, and even in republics, party zeal and a thirst for power, have often induced the establishment of laws which have operated unequally and unjustly.

But in the reign of Christ, it is an important distinction, that all his precepts are framed to have an equal bearing upon every individual.—As all men are the subjects of similar passions and appetites, he requires all to govern themselves by rules which impose like restraints upon all. And that every case may be met by an appropriate rule, he requires those who are surrounded with whatever can afford gratification to the senses, to be temperate in all things—those who have an abundance to be ready to communicate to the wants of the poor—those who are needy, to be reconciled to the will of providence—subjects to honor and obey rulers, and rulers to be upright and faithful, not oppressing the poor nor conniving at the faults of the rich. He commands all men, because all are sinners and liable to endless ruin, to repent and seek the mercy of him who is exalted to bestow pardon upon penitents, and who can give peace to the most distressed conscience, and wash out the deepest stains of guilt. He requires all men, who are made of one blood, to love God as their Creator, with all the heart, and as expecting to leave this world and enter upon eternal scenes, to set their affections upon heavenly things and aspire after "glory, honor, immortality, and eternal life." Here is evidence that the reign of Christ is so pure, that if his laws were fully obeyed, the miseries of the world would be removed, and man would be elevated to great dignity and felicity. These laws have a superior value because they apply immediately to the heart, and require as great purity in men's motives as they do in their actions.

The nature of this kingdom, we may learn, from

II. *The design of Christ's government.*

When earthly princes establish their reigns over nations, they do it, professedly, for the good of their subjects. And this is the design which governments were intended to promote and secure, by their influence in restraining the vicious, in protecting the virtuous, and pointing out the political and civil duties which are necessary to the preservation of civil society and the enjoyment of natural rights. But this design has been too often sacrificed to ambition and pride, till oppressed humanity has risen to shake off the galling yoke, by measures which nothing but despotism could justify. The intention of Christ's reign in the world, is infinitely removed from all such motives, for instead of enriching and ennobling himself, he threw off his native glory, and appeared in the humble form of a servant, and made himself poor, that his subjects might be enriched and dignified. Nor was it possible that "the glory which he had with the Father" before the world was, should be increased by any exertion of his authority among men. He had a right to reign, and that right could not be alienated, though it might be modified by the assumption of the mediatorial office. It is in this view, that Christ's reign appears in the character of pure and disinterested benevolence. Mankind were liable to perish for their rebellion against the throne and government of heaven. But when their exposure was perceived, the Father, moved with infinite pity, (instead of awaking his wrath,) sent forth his Son to propose terms of peace and reconciliation.

When we read that the God of heaven would set up a kingdom in the world, which in the New Testament is called the kingdom of heaven and the kingdom of God, we are to understand that the establishment of the Christian religion is meant—the dominion of our Lord Jesus Christ—the existence of his authority as the highest expression of

Jehovah's love and good will—the character of his influence—the blessings which it imparts to the present life, and the prospect which it holds out of the future.

Let us look at the condition of mankind. Take the map of the world, consider the millions which are crowded upon its surface, and enquire what are their views, their feelings and their conduct toward the author of their being? Do they give evidence of allegiance and fidelity to him whose right it is to reign and with whose reign their highest happiness is intimately connected and should be ever identified? Europe and America afford some traces of loyalty, while Asia and Africa, (if we except a few who have joined the standard of modern missionaries,) oppose themselves in an unbroken column, to his benevolent authority and power. What an affecting view is this! Well may we exclaim with the prophet Jeremiah, " O that my head were waters and mine eyes a fountain of tears, that I might weep day and night for the slain of the daughter of my people!" To recover a revolted and ruined world to loyalty and friendship toward their rightful sovereign, is the object of our Lord's reign. This gracious purpose it proposes to accomplish by exerting a power in their hearts, whose effects shall be seen in an improved life; in dispelling the ignorance, casting down the idols, and removing the miseries which have held an almost undisputed sway over mankind from centu-

ry to century. It is this influence which alone can effectually establish justice, honesty, and benevolence in the world, and which the voice of prediction declares, shall ultimately bless every city, village, and cottage, and raise fallen and degraded man to the favour of his offended God. Does this view look too great to be accomplished? "It is not by might nor by power, but by my spirit saith the Lord of hosts." He is infinitely able to accomplish it and is now rolling on his vast designs with unequal speed, and they must and will roll on till,

"One song employs all nations, and all cry,
"Worthy the Lamb, for he was slain for us.
"The dwellers in the vales and on the rocks,
"Shout to each other, and the mountain tops,
"From distant mountains, catch the flying joy,
"Till nation after nation, taught the strain,
"Earth rolls the rapturous hosanna round."

The government of Jesus Christ is not limited to this transient life, for he came not to sway an earthly sceptre, but to exercise a moral power in the heart, whose influence shall at a brighter day give shape to laws and render human governments, as intended by the Creator, a source of confidence and repose for the protection of every civil and religious right.

All this glory and happiness will be the fruit of his administration, whose benevolence, stretching like the bow in the heavens, shall teach men to estimate every thing by the standard of moral principle, when knowledge and the true spirit of freedom shall prevail over the whole earth.

The nature of this kingdom may be learned from,

III. The *Extent* and *Perpetuity* of Christ's reign.

The kingdoms of this world we know are limited, changeable and perishable. The greatest empires and nations which ever have existed, have reached their zenith of earthly glory, and at length have passed away and been forgotten. In like manner, the greatest kingdoms which now exist will tumble from their elevation, and appear no more. But the kingdom we are directed to pray for, is destined to last forever. "The God of heaven," says the prophet Daniel, "shall set up a kingdom, which shall never be destroyed, and the kingdom shall not be left to other people, but it shall break in pieces and consume all these kingdoms, and it shall stand forever." Unpromising as the fulfilment of this prediction may appear to some, the eye of faith, while it looks to "Jesus Christ, the same yesterday, to day, and forever," will see no obstaele too great to be surmounted, no hindrance that can prevent the complete fulfilment of all that God has spoken. "Why do the heathen rage, and the people imagine a vain thing? The kings of the earth may set themselves, and the rulers of the earth take counsel, against the

Lord, and against his anointed, but he that sitteth in the heavens shall laugh, the Lord shall have them in derision." The same power which attended the first publication of the gospel, subjecting the prejudices of the ignorant, humbling the pride of the learned, and subduing the power of the mighty, will continue to accompany the preaching of the cross, until the dominion of Christ shall "extend from sea even to sea, and from the river unto the ends of the earth."

Whoever industriously studies the prophecies of the scriptures, and candidly reflects upon the present state of the world, must perceive that the march of truth, like a mighty phalanx, is too powerful to be arrested, and that the period is rapidly approaching, when he who "worketh all things after the counsel of his own will," will "cause the wilderness to blossom like the rose, and streams shall break out in the desert;" when the "dark places of the earth shall be enlightened by the bright beams of the Sun of righteousness;" when the "habitations of cruelty" shall become the abodes of meekness and love; when "garments roll'd in blood," and the shouts of the warrior, shall be exchanged for the white robes of peace; and the songs of Zion, when the manacles of Africans shall cease to gall her neglected and oppressed sons, and earth and heaven unite in one voice, crying, "Alleluia, for the Lord God omnipotent reigneth, the kingdoms of the world have become the kingdoms of our Lord and of his Christ."—But whether this golden period be near or far, if the scriptures are our sure guide, the enemies of Jesus will all be humbled, and this King of glory, the "Lord strong and mighty," will triumph and extend his reign till all shall be fulfilled.

In contemplating this animating prospect, the heart of the christian philanthropist swells and beats with joy, while he ardently pours forth, in faith and hope, the prayer of the text, *Thy kingdom come.* But his views are not bounded by the narrow limits of time, however cheering the millennial glory of the world may be; for the kingdom of the Redeemer will last not only as long as this "moving engine" shall exist, but when the great conflagration shall consume the material elements of the universe, and the sun shall be blotted out, this kingdom shall remain unshaken and eternal. The Son of God shall "reign forever and ever," and "all enemies shall be put under his feet."—The last enemy that shall be vanquished is death, that great destroyer who has, for so many ages, stalked and triumphed in the world. Then will the consummation of all things be, when Jesus, the mighty Saviour, having triumphed over all his foes, and gathered all his redeemed to the kingdom prepared for them, shall "deliver up" his mediatorial authority "to God the Father, that God may be all in all." Then shall all the heavenly host say, "Blessing, and honor, and glory, and power, be unto him that sitteth upon the throne, and unto the Lamb forever and ever," while eternal shame and dismay shall be the portion of all his foes.

The subject which has been presented, makes a strong claim upon the candid attention of those, whom the suffrages of a free people have constituted legislators and rulers. As the guardians of the public rights, it is yours to discharge those duties which may conduce to the preservation of the principles recognized by the constitution of this State, that you may be the "ministers of God for good" to the people whose civil interests you are set to guard. Political subjects will necessarily occupy much of your time and attention; and to frame such laws as may promote the public weal, will engross much of your solicitude and care.

It is not my province to point out your duties as statesmen; but as a minister of the gospel, I may be allowed to say, that as you believe the scriptures, and know that "the unrighteous," of whatever class, "shall not inherit the kingdom of God," it is yours to be a "terror to evil doers," and by your example to set yourselves against every corrupt practice, remembering, "that righteousness exalteth a nation, but sin is a reproach to any people." If the measure of men's influence bears a proportion to the elevation of their standing in the community, those who occupy the dignified stations which the providence of God has assigned to *you*, may by a faithful adherence to the principles of integrity and purity, do much to suppress prevalent vices and promote a spirit of genuine regard to morality and piety. And are there no vices to be corrected, vices that are ruinous to the welfare of society, and which require the strong arm of government and faithful example of every good citizen to suppress? The church of God seeks no aid from the civil power, but the quiet enjoyment of her rights; but moral principle in the community, asks the sanction of law in arresting the tide of open profligacy wherever it be found. Were some of the vices prevalent in the world, placed more immediately under the disapprobation of law, and did the public sentiment attach a greater measure of disgrace to the profanation of the sabbath, gambling, profane swearing, and intemperance, we might expect a progress in morals and religion, bearing a just proportion to the increase of wealth and national prosperity.

Suffer me then, venerable rulers, to invite you, so far to make the laws and interests of our Saviour's kingdom an object of your solicitude and *example*, that your influence may contribute to hasten the universal reign of the Prince of peace, when " wisdom and knowledge shall be the stability of the times, and strength of salvation." Is the complete triumph of this reign to be brought about by means of human agency? then it is no less yours than it is every citizen's to impress your sanction upon all the principles and duties which the scriptures inculcate, as fitted to promote sentiments of piety and habits of morality, the best basis on which it is possible the noble structure of our Republic can rest.

As legislators and guardians of the liberties of the people of this State, we tender you our high respects. May you be under the guidance of that wisdom which is profitable to direct, and, with the approbation of your own consciences, enjoy the confidence of the people and the blessing of almighty God.

The subject suggests to the whole assembly, their obligation to God for the period in which we live; and let me remind you, that a prominent feature of the kingdom of Christ is, its power to produce a moral change in the hearts and lives of men. Should you be regardless of the necessity of conversion by the grace of life—should you think lightly of your own guilt as transgressors of the divine law—should feel no necessity for the mediation and atonement of Jesus, be regardless of the pure and benevolent principles of the gospel, and be impenitent and unbelieving,—you must be accounted in the light of enemies who refuse subjection to the authority of Christ.

May God in mercy grant, that in the great day of his wrath, when the "earth and all that therein is, shall be burned up," both rulers and people may be numbered among the faithful subjects of Zion's King—have a shelter beneath the covert of his wings—and be introduced to the beatific presence and everlasting enjoyment of our Lord and Saviour, Jesus Christ. Amen.

Lightning Source UK Ltd.
Milton Keynes UK
UKHW020634080520
362982UK00009B/363